Military Dogs

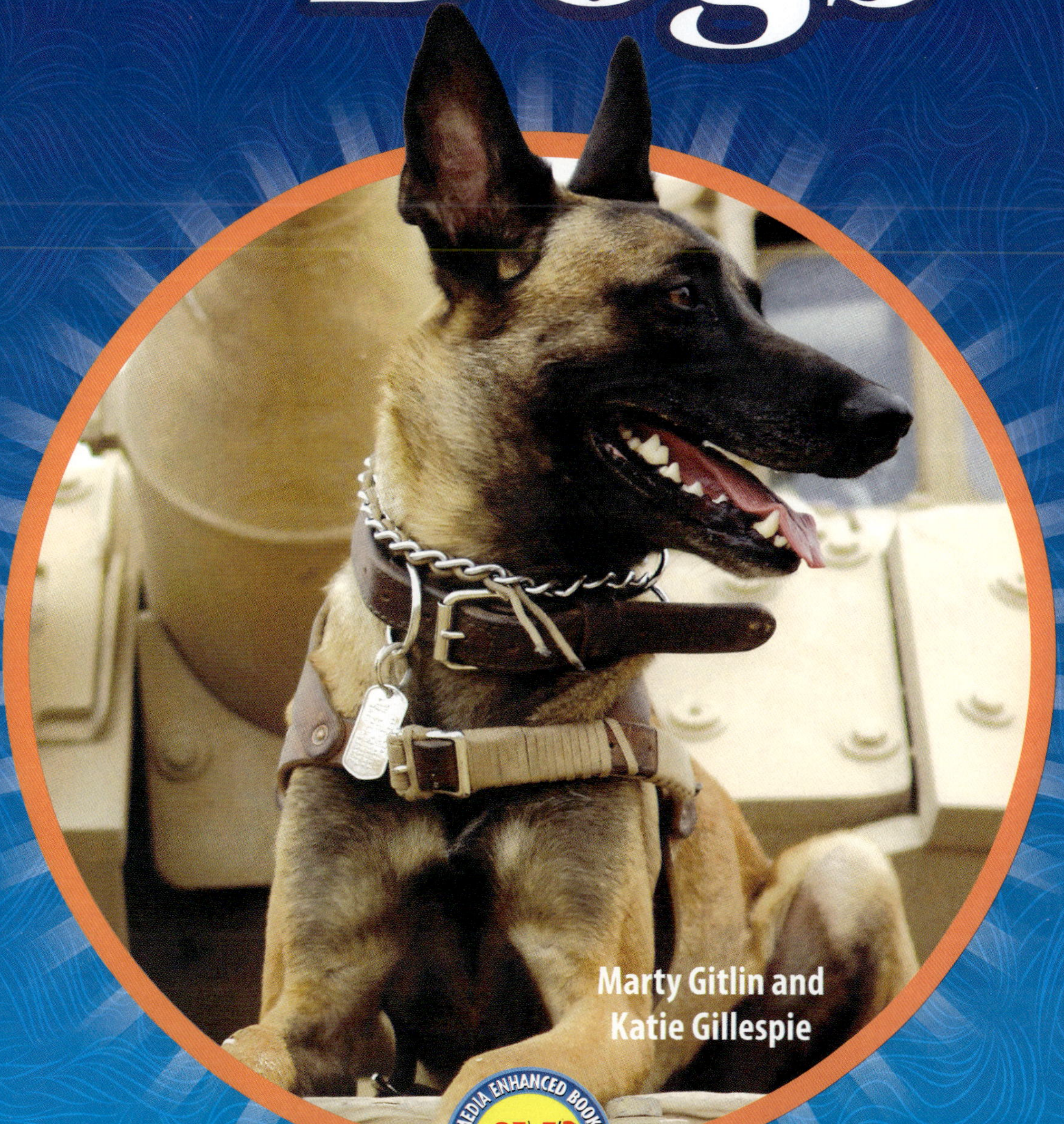

Marty Gitlin and
Katie Gillespie

MEDIA ENHANCED BOOKS
AV2 BY WEIGL
ADDED VALUE • AUDIO VISUAL

www.av2books.com

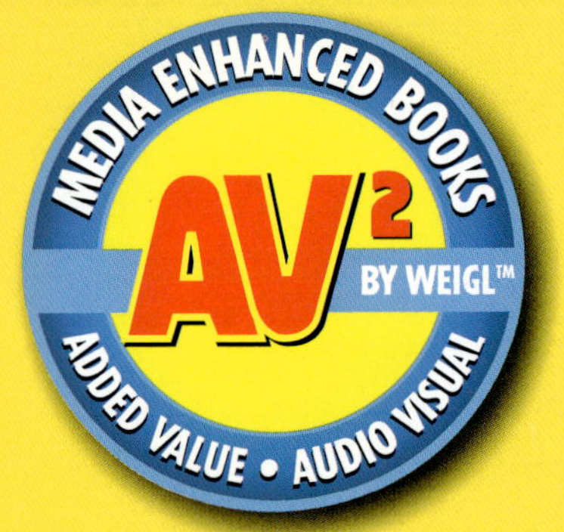

Go to www.av2books.com, and enter this book's unique code.

BOOK CODE

AVU82445

AV² by Weigl brings you media enhanced books that support active learning.

AV² provides enriched content that supplements and complements this book. Weigl's AV² books strive to create inspired learning and engage young minds in a total learning experience.

Your AV² Media Enhanced books come alive with...

Audio
Listen to sections of the book read aloud.

Key Words
Study vocabulary, and complete a matching word activity.

Video
Watch informative video clips.

Quizzes
Test your knowledge.

Embedded Weblinks
Gain additional information for research.

Slide Show
View images and captions, and prepare a presentation.

Try This!
Complete activities and hands-on experiments.

... and much, much more!

Published by AV² by Weigl
350 5th Avenue, 59th Floor
New York, NY 10118
Website: www.av2books.com

Library of Congress Cataloging-in-Publication Data
Names: Gitlin, Marty, author. | Gillespie, Katie, author.
Title: Military dogs / Marty Gitlin and Katie Gillespie.
Description: New York, NY : AV2 by Weigl, [2020] | Series: Dogs with jobs | Audience: Grade 4 to 6. | Includes index.
Identifiers: LCCN 2018053501 (print) | LCCN 2018054201 (ebook) | ISBN 9781489699121 (Multi User Ebook) | ISBN 9781489699138 (Single User Ebook) | ISBN 9781489699107 (hardcover : alk. paper) | ISBN 9781489699114 (softcover : alk. paper)
Subjects: LCSH: Dogs--Military use--Juvenile literature.
Classification: LCC UH100 (ebook) | LCC UH100 .G525 2020 (print) | DDC 355.4/24--dc23
LC record available at https://lccn.loc.gov/2018053501

Printed in Guangzhou, China
1 2 3 4 5 6 7 8 9 0 23 22 21 20 19

012019
103118

Editor: Katie Gillespie Art Director: Terry Paulhus

Weigl acknowledges Getty Images, Alamy, and iStock as its primary image suppliers for this title. Every reasonable effort has been made to trace ownership and to obtain permission to reprint copyright material. The publishers would be pleased to have any errors or omissions brought to their attention so that they may be corrected in subsequent printings.

CONTENTS

Brave Canine Companions

Dogs can be more than just pets. Military dogs have played an important role in the United States armed forces. They help win wars and save lives.

Among their many useful traits is a strong sense of smell. Military dogs have been used to sniff out **bombs** and other weapons. They also track down injured soldiers and even attack enemies.

German shepherds are the most popular breed of military dog. These dogs are chosen because they are smart, athletic, and loyal.

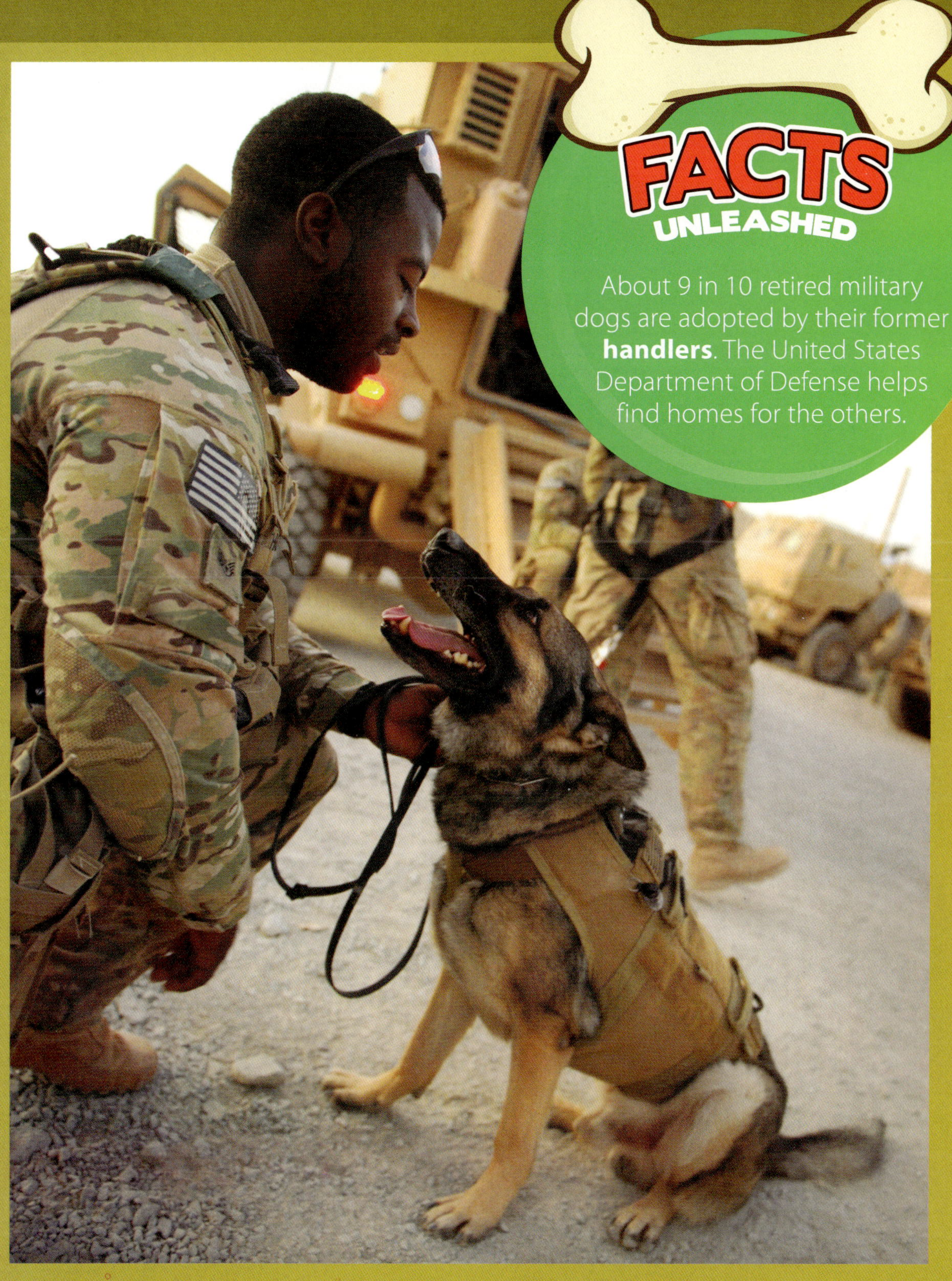

The U.S. military deploys approximately 2,500 war dogs. About 700 serve overseas.

A Long History

The use of war dogs has been traced back more than 2,500 years. The ruler of the ancient Kingdom of Lydia ordered a pack of dogs to attack enemy soldiers. They were very effective against troops mounted on horses. The Roman army also used dogs, centuries later. They bred Molossians to fight in combat.

In the 1500s, Spanish forces conquered land in the New World and placed dogs into battle. They fitted mixed breeds of deerhound and mastiff with spiky collars and padded armor. The huge dogs frightened enemy warriors.

Military dogs were also deployed by British and German forces in World War I. These dogs served as messengers on the front lines and helped detect enemies in the dark. The U.S. military used dogs in World War II. Many families volunteered to give up their pets for the war effort. More than 10,000 dogs served in the war.

Military Dogs Today

Technology has lessened the need for military dogs in war. However, some still serve as **sentry** dogs that watch for enemy movements. They growl and bark to alert troops of a possible attack. Other military canines are taught to keep quiet. **Patrol** dogs make no noises as they hunt snipers and other enemy forces.

Dogs with a keen sense of smell sniff out exploding metal and plastic **land mines**. Their work has resulted in the removal of thousands of mines. It is a very dangerous and important job.

M

Life as a Military Dog

Military dogs do a wide range of tasks. They spend at least one hour each day on **obedience** training. This includes learning how to sit, stay, and heel on command. These dogs also practice biting and searching.

Learning obedience can be fun for the dogs. It allows them to play with their toys and run around. They are not allowed to play with other dogs because they might end up fighting. However, they do play with their handlers.

Military dogs are tired when their daily work is done. They stay in **kennels** overnight to sleep. This helps them refresh for the next day. These special canines serve as both pets and friends to their handlers. They give and receive plenty of love and affection.

Training

Only about 15 in 100 military dogs are born and bred in the United States. The rest are purchased from Germany and the Netherlands. They are sent to the Lackland Air Force Base in San Antonio, Texas. There, they are trained in the Military Working Dog Program.

Military **breeders** pick canines with ideal traits. The dogs must be smart, aggressive, and obedient. They are trained in a variety of tasks by the Army, Navy, Marines, and Air Force.

More than 400 dogs are taught in one of 62 training areas that house 691 kennels. Some are trained in bomb detection. Others learn to sniff out illegal drugs along the border.

All U.S. military dogs and handlers are trained by the 341st Training Squadron. They work in what is known affectionately as the "Dog School." Most dogs become drug or bomb detectors. Some are trained only for patrol use. These dogs are trained more for wartime. They learn how to scout and search for enemy soldiers.

Puppies are also raised as military dogs. They are selected from the time they are born and begin their training at about seven months old. Handlers help them with basic social skills and get them ready for military service.

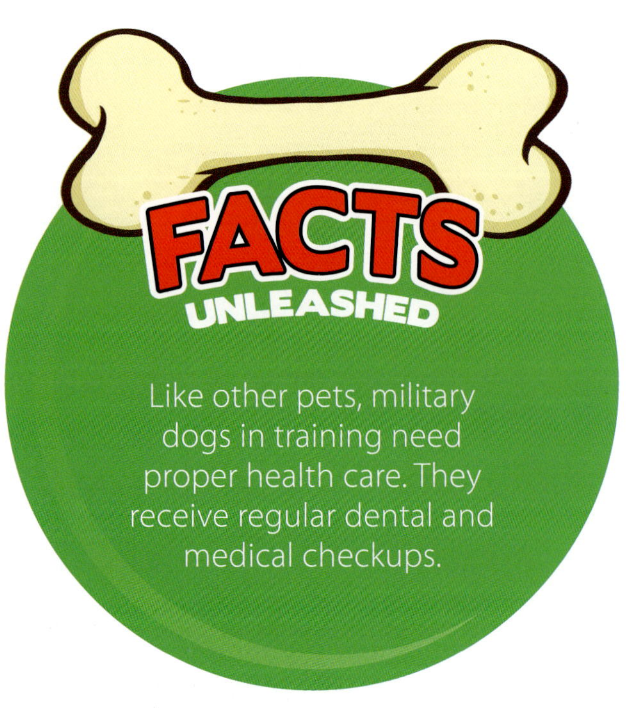

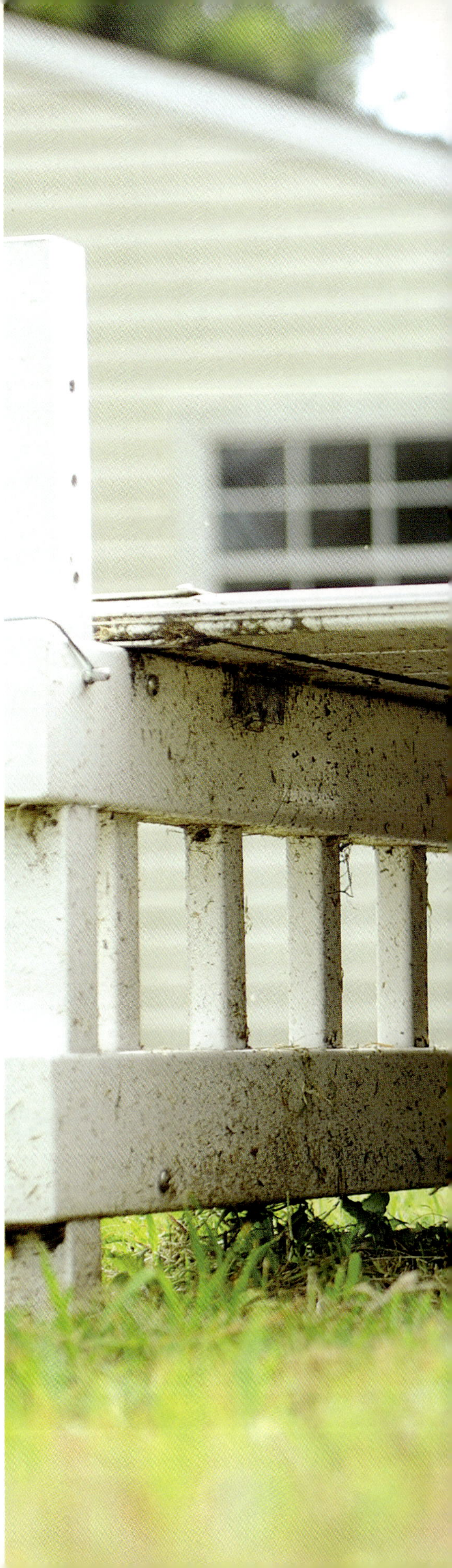

Like other pets, military dogs in training need proper health care. They receive regular dental and medical checkups.

Military Dog Hero: Stubby

Perhaps the most heroic military dog in history was a mixed breed bull terrier named Stubby. He served with the 102nd **Infantry** in the U.S. Army during World War I. Stubby was smuggled into battle by Private J. Robert Conway. He saved lives by detecting enemy gas attacks and barking out warnings of enemy troop movements. Stubby also located wounded soldiers on the battlefield. He even captured a German spy.

The canine hero was honored in a ceremony at the State, War, and Navy Building in Washington, D.C., in 1921. The event was presided over by legendary U.S. general John J. Pershing. He praised Stubby for his heroism and bravery. Pershing pinned a solid gold medal to Stubby's uniform. The dog responded by licking his chops and wagging his tail.

The first canine war hero in the United States was a terrier named Sallie. She served the Union Army during the Civil War. Sallie guarded wounded and dead soldiers.

Stubby was nominated for the rank of sergeant by the commanding general of the 102nd Infantry. Although he may not have officially received this rank, he was known as Sgt. Stubby from then on. Stubby was even presented with a medal by the French.

Stubby's work had a lasting effect. He opened people's eyes to the value of dogs in wartime. Stubby convinced military leaders to use canines, mostly for scouting, in World War II.

WORK HARD
UNDER
GO
BOYS

Meeting Military Dogs

Military dogs are trained to be aggressive. Typically, they should not be approached, especially by children. For safety reasons, retired military dogs cannot be adopted by families with children under five years of age.

Kids often stand at eye level with large dogs. They must avoid making sudden movements, such as reaching out to pet the dog. Although handlers keep a firm grip on their animals, they can bite quickly.

What Makes a Good Military Dog?

Many traits are necessary for a dog to succeed in the military. This is why about half of all dogs drop out of the training program. Military dogs must be aggressive and smart. They should also learn commands quickly and be able to carry them out effectively.

Military dogs require physical talents such as speed and strength. They should be willing to attack if threatened. Some dogs are dismissed from military service because they become too stressed at the idea of biting a human.

Quiz

1 Which breed of military dog is the most popular?

2 What kind of military dogs make no noise as they hunt snipers?

3 Where do dogs in training stay overnight?

4 What two countries breed the most military dogs?

5 Why are dogs in training not allowed to play with other dogs?

6 In what state is Lackland Air Force Base?

7 In which war did Stubby serve?

8 Where were military dogs first used?

9 What sense do dogs use to track down bombs and mines?

10 What country used dogs to conquer territory in the 1500s?

ANSWERS

1 German shepherd **2** Patrol dogs **3** Kennels **4** Germany and the Netherlands **5** Because they might fight **6** Texas **7** World War I **8** Lydia **9** Sense of smell **10** Spain

Key Words

bombs: devices filled with incendiary materials designed to explode on impact

breeders: people who work to develop ideal skills for military dogs

handlers: people who work with military dogs

infantry: army soldiers that fight on foot

kennels: shelter for military dogs

land mines: explosive mines laid just below the ground's surface

obedience: the act of following orders

patrol: to keep watch over an area

sentry: a soldier who is stationed to stand guard

Index

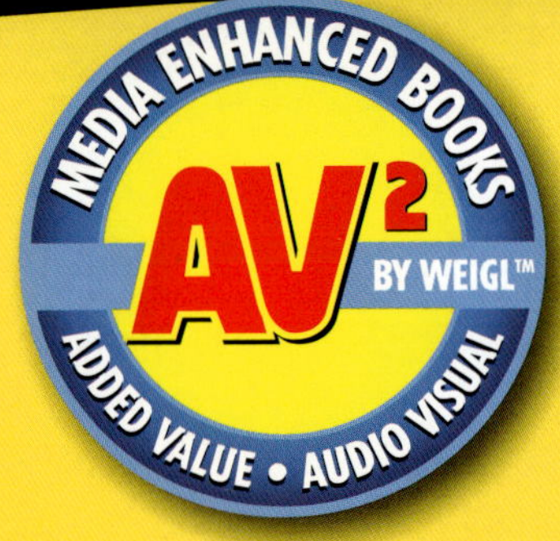

Log on to www.av2books.com

AV² by Weigl brings you media enhanced books that support active learning. Go to www.av2books.com, and enter the special code found on page 2 of this book. You will gain access to enriched and enhanced content that supplements and complements this book. Content includes video, audio, weblinks, quizzes, a slide show, and activities.

AV² Online Navigation

Audio
Listen to sections of the book read aloud.

Book Pages
AV² pages directly correspond to pages in the book.

Video
Watch informative video clips.

Embedded Weblinks
Gain additional information for research.

Key Words
Study vocabulary, and complete a matching word activity.

Try This!
Complete activities and hands-on experiments.

Quizzes
Test your knowledge.

Slide Show
View images and captions, and prepare a presentation.

AV² was built to bridge the gap between print and digital. We encourage you to tell us what you like and what you want to see in the future.

Sign up to be an AV² Ambassador at www.av2books.com/ambassador.

Due to the dynamic nature of the Internet, some of the URLs and activities provided as part of AV² by Weigl may have changed or ceased to exist. AV² by Weigl accepts no responsibility for any such changes. All media enhanced books are regularly monitored to update addresses and sites in a timely manner. Contact AV² by Weigl at 1-866-649-3445 or av2books@weigl.com with any questions, comments, or feedback.